CW01191616

WINNERSH PRIMARY SCHOOL

WORLD OF FOOD

For Mum, who taught me that cooking could be fun – S.L.

To Mercedes, who ate most of the dishes from the book with me.
For research purposes – V.N.

A TEMPLAR BOOK

First published in the UK in 2022 by Templar Books,
an imprint of Bonnier Books UK
4th Floor, Victoria House,
Bloomsbury Square, London WC1B 4DA
Owned by Bonnier Books
Sveavägen 56, Stockholm, Sweden
www.bonnierbooks.co.uk

Text copyright © 2022 by Sandra Lawrence
Illustration copyright © 2022 by Violeta Noy
Design copyright © 2022 by Templar Books

1 3 5 7 9 10 8 6 4 2

All rights reserved

ISBN 978-1-78741-743-4

This book was typeset in Giulia Plain,
Graham Bold and Extra Grotesque.
The illustrations were created digitally.

Consulted by Dr Jakob Klein
Edited by Carly Blake and Katie Haworth
Designed by Ted Jennings and Olivia Cook
Production Controller Neil Randles

Printed in Latvia

MIX
Paper from
responsible sources
FSC® C002795

WORLD OF FOOD

Written by **SANDRA LAWRENCE**
Illustrated by **VIOLETA NOY**

templar
books

WORLD OF FOOD

Contents

WHAT WE NEED TO EAT 6
THE BEGINNING OF CUISINE 8
ANCIENT ROMAN BANQUETS 10
WHERE FOOD COMES FROM 12

◆

TERRIFIC TUBERS 14
THE VEGETABLE GARDEN 16
FRUITS AND NUTS 18
A FEAST OF FUNGI 20
AROUND THE WORLD: FRUITS AND VEGETABLES ... 22

◆

A CORNUCOPIA OF CORN 24
RICE OF LIFE 26
LET'S EAT WHEAT 27
AROUND THE WORLD: GRAINS AND CEREALS 28

◆

MIGHTY MILK 30
THE STORY OF CHEESE 32
BUTTER 34
EGGS 35
AROUND THE WORLD: DAIRY AND EGGS 36

WORLD OF FOOD

ALL ABOUT MEAT 38
FISH AND SEAFOOD 40
AROUND THE WORLD: MEAT AND SEAFOOD 42

◆

SALT AND PEPPER 44
HOT, HOT CHILLIES 45
HERBS AND SPICES 46

◆

HONEY 48
SUGAR 49
CHOCOLATE 50
AROUND THE WORLD: SWEETS 52

◆

FESTIVE FOODS 54–57
THE TRICKY QUESTIONS 58
THE FUTURE OF FOOD 60

◆

GLOSSARY 62
BREAD RECIPE 64

WHAT WE NEED TO EAT

Eating gives us energy to fuel our muscles, organs and brain, as well as the nutrients to keep our cells growing, our bodies repaired and our immune systems healthy. We use the word 'nutrition' to explain the different ways that food affects us physically. A balanced diet is one where we get enough of everything our bodies need to function, and it can help us feel our best, too.

Eating a variety of different foods is good for us. This plate is a good guide for a balanced diet.

Protein is found in nuts, seeds, beans, grains, meat, fish, seafood, eggs and milk.

PROTEIN

Protein is a nutrient that gives our bodies molecules called 'amino acids'. These molecules are like building blocks, and connect together to build muscle tissue and repair organs such as the brain and skin. They also help in transporting oxygen around the body in our blood and fighting off infections.

*Around a quarter of our diet should be **protein**.*

*Around a quarter of our diet should be starchy complex **carbohydrates**.*

Complex carbohydrates are found in foods like bread, pasta, potatoes, rice and corn.

CARBOHYDRATES

Carbohydrates provide us with daily fuel. They are easily turned into sugar (glucose) that can directly enter our bloodstream for instant energy. The body will either use the energy straight away or store it for later. 'Simple carbohydrates', found in sugar, fruit juice and sweets, give an immediate burst of energy but it doesn't last long. It's better to eat 'complex carbohydrates', such as potatoes, because the body takes longer to break them down, so they continue giving us energy for longer.

FATS

We need fats because they supply the body with a very concentrated form of energy. This is measured in 'calories'. Fat also gives structure to the cells of the body, keeps it insulated against the cold, and helps lubricate and cushion the bones and other organs.

Fats are vital to our health, but they should be eaten in moderation. Fried foods and chocolate bars are high in fat and oil, so you should only eat them in small amounts, if at all. Foods such as nuts and avocados contain natural fats and are healthier options.

Fats are found in nuts, seeds, avocados, plant-based oils such as sunflower and olive oil, butter, meats, cheese and oily fish.

Around half our diet should be **fruits and vegetables**. Different coloured vegetables contain different **vitamins** and **minerals**.

VITAMINS

Vitamins help our bodies perform hundreds of tasks, from energy production to repairing cells and forming bones.

Vitamin A is good for our eyesight and skin. It also boosts the body's immune system to help fight off infection. It is found in dairy foods, oily fish, leaves, orange vegetables and fruits.

There are several types of **B vitamins**, and each one helps a different part of the body to function. Eggs, beans and dark-leaved vegetables contain all the B vitamins.

Vitamin C keeps the body's cells healthy, including our skin, blood vessels, bone and cartilage. It also helps wounds to heal. It is found in lots of fruits and vegetables, especially citrus fruits.

Iron is found in beans, nuts, green, leafy vegetables and meat. Calcium is found in dairy produce such as cheese and milk, as well as leafy vegetables and some nuts and legumes.

MINERALS

Like vitamins, minerals are nutrients that our bodies need in small amounts to function well.

Minerals include:

Iron: This is important for red blood cells, which carry oxygen around the body.

Calcium: This mineral keeps our bones and teeth strong, and helps the body with many other tasks, too.

THE BEGINNING OF CUISINE

The very earliest humans hunted animals and gathered wild plants but they had to eat everything raw. When people learned how to control fire, however, everything changed. They had invented cooking.

STONE-AGE DIET

The ancestors of modern humans may have used fire to cook meat 1.8 million years ago. Cooked meat was easier to digest, which made it more nutritious than raw meat. Cooking it also made it less likely to make people ill, but, best of all, it added tasty flavour. Eating was no longer just about refuelling the body – it was something people did for enjoyment.

Ötzi the iceman

ÖTZI THE ICEMAN

Ötzi the iceman lived 5,300 years ago, and his body was preserved in ice in the European Alps. We know a lot about his diet from his remains. His final meal included…

Wild goat

Red deer

Einkorn wheat

Particles of charcoal suggest the meat Ötzi ate was cooked or smoked to preserve it.

FOSSILISED FOOD

Archaeologists can often work out what prehistoric people ate by studying remains left in cooking pots and even analysing fossilised poo! In Britain around 6000 BCE, people enjoyed nettle pudding and roast hedgehog.

EARLY FARMING

Goats, sheep, chickens, cattle and pigs were domesticated from about 10,000 years ago. Farming plants also probably began about the same time in the Fertile Crescent – an area in the Middle East that includes modern Iran, Iraq, Turkey and Syria.

GROWING CROPS

Agriculture developed independently in many parts of the world, including China, India, New Guinea, West Africa, Mexico and the Andes Mountains in South America. Early crops included wheat (see page 27), barley, lentils, flaxseed and chickpeas.

INVENTING FOR FOOD

Many early technologies were designed to make the gathering, production, preparation or storage of food easier.

The earliest pottery shards date from around 20,000 years ago and were found in Central China. Pottery was useful for storing food and cooking.

Around 30,000 years ago, Indigenous Australians found that if they ground wild grain between two stones they could mix it with water and bake it to make bread.

The oldest-known fishing net was found in the town of Antrea, Finland, in 1913, and it has been carbon-dated to 8540 BCE.

The oldest written recipes can be found on clay tablets dating from around 1750 BCE. They are written in a text called cuneiform, used by the ancient Mesopotamians.

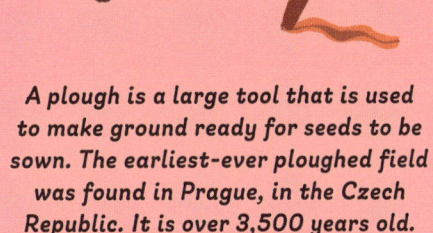

A plough is a large tool that is used to make ground ready for seeds to be sown. The earliest-ever ploughed field was found in Prague, in the Czech Republic. It is over 3,500 years old.

Early ovens were 'pit ovens', dug into the ground and lined with stones. One early example is in Mezhirich, Ukraine. It dates to 20,000 BCE, and was used to cook mammoth!

ANCIENT ROMAN BANQUETS

In ancient times, like today, people loved to celebrate with fancy food. In Rome, wealthy people enjoyed banquets so much they painted pictures of them on their walls. Archaeologists have found ancient Roman cookbooks and have even excavated the remains of the food itself. At its height, the Roman Empire spanned much of Europe and parts of North Africa and West Asia. Rome was supplied with food from around the Empire and beyond.

A ROMAN FEAST

Cena was a celebratory meal or banquet. It often had three elaborate courses served in a *triclinium*, or formal dining room. Diners did not sit upright, but laid down on low couches to eat. The guests were served by household slaves.

Lots of fish was eaten, and wealthy guests might have dined on exotic swordfish.

Sauces were strong-smelling and strong-tasting, made with salt, vinegar, spices and herbs. Garum was a pungent, salty sauce made from fermented fish innards. The Romans used it on many foods.

Snails or cochleas were soaked in milk and salt, and then fried in oil to eat.

Few Romans liked beef, but they did eat hare, chicken, pheasant, lamb and pork. Wild boar was highly valued and often eaten at lavish banquets.

Wine, olive oil and **garum** were kept in tall terracotta jars called *amphorae*.

RICH AND POOR

Wealthy Romans may have enjoyed exotic delicacies but the poor had much less delicious food. They had to make do with porridge called *pulmentaria* and vegetables such as lentils and onions. Many slaves ate shellfish and filled up with coarse, dry bread made from barley.

It was considered polite to belch. It showed you'd enjoyed the meal!

Olives were extremely important, both as food and pressed into olive oil.

Nuts included walnuts, hazelnuts and almonds.

Edible dormice were about the size of squirrels. Chefs kept them in a special 'fattening jar' called a *glirarium* and fed them on nuts. When the dormice were big enough, they were killed, stuffed with minced pork and baked.

Only the rich could afford fine **white bread** made with refined wheat flour.

Honey was used to sweeten dishes. The Romans did not have sugar.

Sausages or *farcimina* were extremely popular, and whole chapters of cookbooks were devoted to their preparation.

The Romans loved **fruits** such as apples, peaches, grapes, pomegranates, plums, pears and especially figs.

WHERE FOOD COMES FROM

Fruits, vegetables and other food crops don't always originate from the places where they are grown today. Many of the foods we eat every day were first cultivated on just one continent or island for thousands of years before they were spread by trade or migration.

NEW FOODS

When Europeans first went to the Americas, they brought many foods back, including potatoes, tomatoes and corn.

This map shows where some of the foods we are familiar with originally came from.

SWEET POTATOES

The sweet potato, or *kumara* as it is known in New Zealand, originally came from South America. Around 1000 CE it is thought that Polynesian sailors travelling from the Pacific Islands picked up sweet potatoes in South America, then journeyed on to New Zealand.

TRAVELLING APPLES

Some people think apples may have been brought from Asia to Europe by traders travelling along the Silk Road who ate the fruits and threw the cores away.

FAR AND WIDE

Some foods grow wild in more than one region. That's because the land has shifted. Over millions of years, the continents moved apart, and some countries that are now separated were once joined together. Back then, animals and weather conditions would have helped spread seeds.

FOOD CROPS

Millet and sorghum are cereal crops – types of grasses that produce edible seeds, or grain. Different species of millet come from Africa, the Middle East and China. Sorghum probably originated in Africa and spread around the globe.

TERRIFIC TUBERS

Some plants develop starchy growths, called tubers, on their roots to store nutrients for winter. Our ancestors quickly discovered that these tubers tasted good and they have been a vital food source for thousands of years.

THE HUMBLE POTATO

Potatoes originate from South America. People in modern-day Peru and Bolivia started growing them by 5000 BCE and possibly as early as 10,000 BCE. In the sixteenth century, Spanish conquistadors introduced potatoes to Europe. At first, Europeans thought the knobbly vegetables were poisonous, but they soon discovered that they were easy to grow, filling and could be cooked in lots of different ways.

In the eighteenth century, King Louis XVI of France and his wife, Marie Antoinette, wore potato flowers in their clothes. This encouraged French farmers to grow the new crop.

THE POTATO FAMINE

The humble potato changed the course of history. In the 1840s and 1850s, a disease called blight started to attack potatoes. A mould covered the vegetables with purple spots, making them rot in the fields. In some countries in Europe at this time poor people relied on potatoes for food. The potato famine had a devastating effect, especially in Ireland. Here, one million people died and another million left the country. This migration continued for decades, with four million people leaving the country in the 50 years after the famine.

POTATO DISHES AROUND THE WORLD

Potatoes are very versatile and can be cooked in almost any way. It seems every country has its own favourite dish.

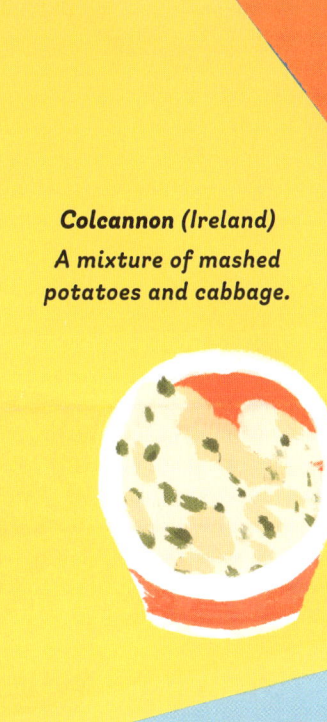

Colcannon (Ireland)
A mixture of mashed potatoes and cabbage.

Gnocchi (Italy)
Potato dumplings that are eaten with a variety of sauces.

Chips and fries
Sliced and deep-fried potatoes are enjoyed around the world.

Gamjajeon (Korea)
Fried savoury pancakes made with grated or ground potatoes.

Gratin dauphinois (France)
Thinly sliced potatoes baked in milk or cream.

Hash browns (USA)
Fried shredded potatoes.

Saag aloo (India)
Spiced potatoes with spinach.

OTHER TUBERS WE EAT

Potatoes aren't the only tubers we eat. Jerusalem artichokes and dahlias have edible tuberous roots and some other tubers are even more popular than potatoes in parts of the world.

Cassava, also known as manioc or yuca, is a woody, brown tuber. It was originally from South America. Today, it is a staple food for nearly one billion people around the world. Many people cook with tapioca, a starch extracted from the cassava plant.

Yams come from Africa, Asia and the Caribbean. Their long, brown tubers are traditionally boiled or roasted. They can be white, yellow, pink and purple, and can taste sweet or bitter.

Unrelated to the regular potato or the yam, **sweet potato** is a sweet-tasting tuber full of fibre, vitamins and minerals. It is popular around the world.

Kat-kat manioc is a stew from Mauritius made with green vegetables, beans and cassava.

Yam is a classic base for **fufu**, a dish made of pounded starchy vegetables. Fufu originates in West Africa and is also found in the Caribbean.

In Korea, **gun-goguma** (roasted sweet potatoes) are baked in big drums by street vendors in winter. They taste sweet and nutty.

THE VEGETABLE GARDEN

We eat different parts of plants according to what they taste like and how nutritious they are. Tasty tubers like potatoes grow underground on roots, but we also eat seeds, bulbs, shoots, roots, stems, leaves, buds, fruits and even flowers. Gardeners and farmers grow a variety of vegetables so that there is fresh food to eat all year round.

SHOOTS AND STEMS

Shoots and stems are often crunchy and delicious. Celery is a stem that is used in salads and to flavour soups. The shoots of mung beans, known as 'beansprouts', and bamboo are both popular in South and Southeast Asia.

Queen Nefertiti of ancient Egypt described asparagus as 'food of the gods'. We eat the young stems of the asparagus plant.

Mung beans

Celery

Rocket

TASTY LEAVES

We eat a huge variety of leaves, from salad crops, such as lettuce and rocket, to brassicas, such as cabbages and nutrient-rich spinach.

Cabbage

Lettuce

Spinach

Garlic

Fennel

Leek

Spring onion

White onion

Red onion

BULBS BELOW

The *Allium* family of plants, which includes onions and garlic, store goodness in their bulbs to feed a young plant in the first months of its life. They are often very strongly flavoured, which makes them extremely good in cooking.

Onions are the second most popular vegetable on Earth!

LOTS OF LEGUMES

Legumes are a family of plants with edible seeds that contain protein and nutrients. They include peas, beans, lentils and chickpeas, which are important foods all around the world. They can be dried to preserve them or eaten fresh. Pulses are the dried seeds of legumes.

Soybeans

Lentils

Cucumbers

Squashes

Peppers

Peas

Green beans

Soybeans are used in so many foods that you might not realise you're eating them! Bread and chocolate contain soy, as well as soy sauce, soy milk and tofu (bean curd).

Artichokes

Poppies

Artichokes are a member of the thistle family. Their flower buds are tough on the outside but tender and tasty inside.

SURPRISE!

Many 'vegetables' we eat are actually fruits (see page 18) in botanical terms. These include tomatoes, peppers, cucumbers and squashes.

Courgettes

Sunflower

Tomatoes

EDIBLE FLOWERS

Some vegetables are actually flowers! Brussels sprouts are individual flower buds, and cauliflower and broccoli are clusters of hundreds of tiny buds. We also eat the seeds of many flowers, including sunflowers and poppies. Some seeds, including canola and sesame, are used to make oil.

Brussels sprouts

Cauliflower

Broccoli

Turnip

White radish

Radish

Beetroot

Carrot

NUTRITIOUS ROOTS

Some plants have thick, straight 'taproots'. These store nutrients for the plant, such as slow-burning carbohydrates, vitamins and minerals. Those nutrients are good for us, too.

Over hundreds of years, farmers have bred roots to grow bigger and to look nicer. Wild carrots were once purple and yellow, but Dutch growers developed the orange version in the sixteenth and seventeenth centuries.

FRUITS AND NUTS

One of the most common ways for plants to reproduce is by making seeds. Plants put a lot of energy into producing seeds, so they need to keep them safe with protective casings. Some seeds have soft outer casings – we know these as fruits.

A flower is the reproductive part of a plant. Stamens are the male organs and they produce pollen. Ovaries are the female organs and they contain ovules.

MANY BERRIES

In botany, berries are fruits that grow from a single ovary on a plant and do not have a stone. As well as blueberries and cranberries, grapes, bananas, kiwis, lychees and papaya are all berries, too. So are citrus fruits like oranges, lemons and limes.

After a flower has been pollinated, usually by insects, the ovules develop into seeds and the ovaries develop into fruits.

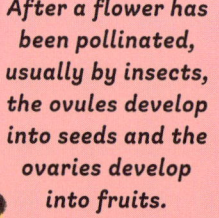

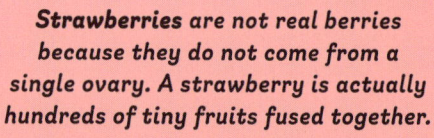

Strawberries *are not real berries because they do not come from a single ovary. A strawberry is actually hundreds of tiny fruits fused together.*

Loquats *are small, yellow citrus fruits originally from East Asia.*

POMES APLENTY

Pomes are a type of fruit that have a fleshy outer part and a tougher core containing the seed. Apples, pears, quinces and loquats are all examples of pomes.

DELICIOUS DRUPES

Drupes are fruits from a single ovary with a single, large seed. Peaches, cherries, mangoes and olives are all drupes.

PRIZED PINEAPPLES

Pineapples are the only member of the bromeliad family of plants that has an edible fruit. They need a very warm climate to grow and originally came from South America but were brought to Europe by conquistadors. In the seventeenth and eighteenth centuries, pineapples became a status symbol in Europe, as wealthy people built expensive hot houses to grow them in. Today, pineapples are still grown in the UK, in the Lost Gardens of Heligan in Cornwall.

Sometimes drupes are gathered together in clusters, including raspberries and blackberries (more berries that aren't true berries).

TOUGH NUTS

Nuts are hard-shelled fruits with the seed attached inside.

Despite its name, a coconut is not a nut but a drupe! The white flesh of coconuts is used to flavour both sweet and savoury dishes. Coconut milk (the creamy liquid made from grating the coconut flesh and adding water) is used in sauces.

Peanuts are actually legumes, from the pea and bean family. Unlike true nuts, peanuts develop underground.

Across the world we eat more than 100 million tonnes of watermelons every year. They grow in dry areas where many other fruits can't survive.

WE EAT THE MOST...

Tomatoes and bananas! After tomatoes, bananas are the world's most consumed fruit. Their larger, savoury relatives, known as plantains, are very common in Caribbean cooking and make up 0.3 per cent of the world's food supply.

A FEAST OF FUNGI

Fungi are neither animals nor plants, but a life form in their own right. They are so diverse that we sometimes don't even realise we are eating them. From yeasts, which are microscopic, to the larger organisms that produce mushrooms, fungi can live anywhere, including in soil, water, plants, animals and even the air!

ANCIENT FUNGI

People have been eating mushrooms since the Stone Age. Archaeologists excavating the 18,700-year-old grave of the Red Lady of El Miron, in Spain, discovered that she had eaten red deer, ibex, salmon – and mushrooms – making her the world's first-known fungi fan!

Red Lady of El Miron

MUSHROOMS

We usually eat the reproductive part of a fungus, called the 'fruiting body' or mushroom. No one knows how many types of fungus there are – estimates vary and new species are being discovered all the time. What we do know, however, is that about 350 species are gathered for food.

Bright orange 'chicken of the woods' grows on tree trunks in Northern Europe and North America. It has been foraged for centuries and is cooked in similar ways to meat.

Button mushrooms are often found in the supermarket. They are usually cultivated (grown especially) but can also be found growing wild in North America and Europe.

Black truffles are one of the most expensive foods in the world. They grow underground and truffle hunters use specially trained pigs or dogs to sniff them out.

Porcini are popular in France and Italy for their rich, nutty flavour. These mushrooms are hard to farm, so they have to be gathered from the wild.

Enoki mushrooms look like tiny bunches of creamy-white berries on stalks. They are widely used in Chinese, Japanese and other South Asian cuisine, and stay crunchy even when cooked.

Kalahari truffles, also known as 'African potatoes', grow in the Namibian desert. They are milder in flavour than black truffles. They can be boiled as a side dish, used to flavour butter, and are sometimes eaten sweetened in ice cream.

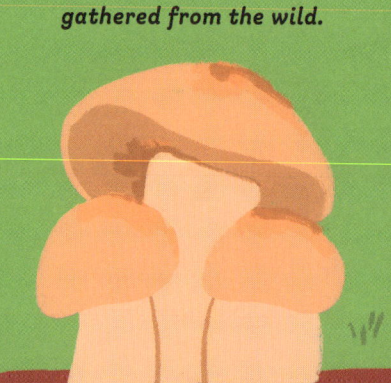

BEWARE WHAT YOU PICK!

Fungi grow wild in lots of places and they can be highly nutritious and tasty to eat. In some countries, such as Italy, the mushroom-gathering season is a big event. Families pass down knowledge from generation to generation of the 'secret' places where the best varieties can be found growing wild. However, some species are highly toxic to humans, and only experienced adults should gather them from the wild. Sometimes poisonous and edible mushrooms look very similar.

*Many wild mushroom recipes are simple, like Italian porcini **risotto**. Using few ingredients brings out the flavour of the porcini mushrooms.*

Morel — EDIBLE
False Morel — POISONOUS

*Sukiyaki is a Japanese **nabi**, or hot-pot dish, usually cooked at the table. Mushrooms are a key ingredient, along with tofu and noodles.*

USEFUL YEAST

Yeast is a single-celled microorganism that rapidly reproduces in hot, wet conditions. It converts sugars and starch into bubbles of carbon dioxide and alcohol, creating a froth, in a process called 'fermentation'. Humans started using the products of this process thousands of years ago to make bread and beer.

Brewer's yeast is used to make beer frothy.

*Today, **baker's yeast** is added to a flour-and-water mixture, and the gas bubbles in the mixture make the bread rise. This strengthens the dough and adds its own special flavour. Bread dough is left in a warm place to prove (double in size) before it is baked. We're not sure exactly when or where bread was invented, but archaeologists have found evidence of leavened (risen) bread in Egypt dating back to around 1000 BCE.*

One of the earliest known poems is called the Hymn to Ninkasi. It dates from around 1800 BCE and is about the Sumerian goddess of beer. In ancient Mesopotamia, beer was brewed by priestesses.

AROUND THE WORLD: FRUITS AND VEGETABLES

Neeps and tatties is a dish of mashed swedes and potatoes. On Burns Night (25 January), which celebrates the famous Scottish poet Robert Burns, it is often eaten with haggis (see page 42).

Tanghulu is a sweet snack made from Chinese hawthorn fruits dipped in sweet syrup and threaded onto bamboo sticks. In Northern China it has been eaten for nearly 1,000 years.

Ćwikła is a mixture of grated beetroot and horseradish. It is a popular side dish in Poland, often served with sausage and ham at Easter.

In Russia, **potatoes and mushrooms** are often fried together to make a filling, warm meal.

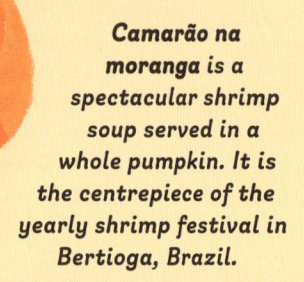

Camarão na moranga is a spectacular shrimp soup served in a whole pumpkin. It is the centrepiece of the yearly shrimp festival in Bertioga, Brazil.

Mofongo is a dish from Puerto Rico and the Dominican Republic. Similar to fufu from West Africa, it is made with pounded plantains. It was originally created in the Caribbean by enslaved African people and their descendants.

Sukuma wiki means 'stretch the week' in Swahili. It is a Kenyan dish of spicy greens, rice and tomatoes and it gets its name because it is a tasty, filling way to stretch ingredients to last longer!

Edamame is Japanese for 'beans on a branch'. Only the beans are eaten, but they are cooked in their pods because they add flavour.

Frijoles refritos or 'refried beans' are a staple dish in Mexican cuisine. The beans are not fried twice, but the dish's English name comes from the Spanish word for 'really well-fried'.

Shakshuka is a Middle Eastern and North African breakfast dish of poached eggs cooked with tomatoes, chilli, onion and cumin, served in the cast-iron pan it was cooked in.

For centuries in Korea, people have preserved vegetables by salting and fermenting them. The first **kimchi** was made with radishes. Today, the most popular type is made from cabbage.

Peanut butter is a popular spread in North America, often eaten on toast for breakfast. The Incas and Aztecs ate ground, roasted peanuts. The peanut butter we know today was first made in Canada in 1884.

Dal is the Indian name for dried split beans and pulses. They are often prepared with delicious spices to make a thick, hearty dish with the same name.

Strudel means 'whirlpool' in German. Classic Austrian apple strudel is a swirl of pastry with slices of apple and cinnamon paste.

A CORNUCOPIA OF CORN

Popcorn, corn on the cob or tasty cornbread – corn is delicious! Corn, also called maize, is a member of the grass family. Today, it makes up around one-fifth of the world's diet and it has some other handy uses, too.

INCA AND AZTEC DIETS

Indigenous Central Americans first domesticated teosinte grass around 10,000 years ago. Over time, the people bred the grass to have giant ears (stem tips), each with hundreds of tiny kernels (seeds). This food became extremely important in Inca and Aztec diets. When Europeans first arrived in the Americas in the fifteenth century, they were introduced to maize.

Sweetcorn is a type of corn that is high in sugar and tastes delicious cooked and eaten straight from the cob.

THE THREE SISTERS

Corn, beans and squash make up the trio of crops known as the 'Three Sisters'. They have been at the centre of Native American agriculture and cuisine for centuries. The farmers planted the crops together, so the tall maize stems would support the climbing beans and the large squash leaves would shade the soil, helping to keep moisture in.

Tortillas are flatbreads made from maize flour, though they were once made from simmered corn kernels. They came from Mexico where they are a staple food.

LEGENDS

There are dozens of legends about corn amongst Native American peoples across North, South and Central America.

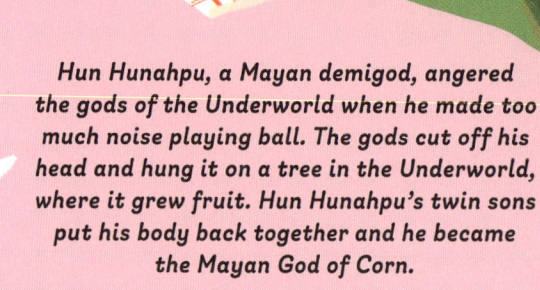

Hun Hunahpu, a Mayan demigod, angered the gods of the Underworld when he made too much noise playing ball. The gods cut off his head and hung it on a tree in the Underworld, where it grew fruit. Hun Hunahpu's twin sons put his body back together and he became the Mayan God of Corn.

CORN AND VAMPIRES

Christopher Columbus brought the first cobs of corn to Europe in 1493. Even though people in Europe were suspicious of this new food, some of the poorest came to rely on it. However, they didn't know how to prepare it to get the nutrients their bodies needed, so they sometimes got a disease called pellagra. Pellagra victims became sensitive to light, had trouble sleeping and developed bleeding sores on their mouths. It's believed some people thought they were vampires!

Cornflakes were invented by American food manufacturer John Harvey Kellogg in 1898, during a failed attempt to make granola. They are a popular breakfast food in some parts of the world, often eaten with milk.

CONCEALED CORN

Corn can be processed into a surprisingly large range of ingredients and it is used in many basic dishes.

Corn oil is used for cooking.

Corn starch is a fine flour used for thickening sauces and stews.

Maize syrup uses the fructose (sugar) in corn as a sweetener. It appears in many foods, but like sugar (page 49), it is not healthy in large amounts.

Popcorn is made by toasting dried kernels until they explode. The earliest popcorn discovered was found in New Mexico in the United States. It is over 4,000 years old!

POWERED BY CORN

Corn can also be used to produce ethanol, a biofuel, which can power a car. Although it might seem like a good idea to use biofuel, which releases fewer carbon emissions than fossil fuels such as coal and oil, it can have negative consequences for people and the planet. The fertilisers used to grow the huge quantities of corn pollute natural ecosystems and sometimes wild spaces are cleared to grow it.

25

RICE OF LIFE

People began to cultivate rice 13,500 to 8,000 years ago in Asia, from a wild grass called *Oryza rufipogon*. The grain gradually spread throughout the world, and today it makes up around 15 per cent of the calories humans eat.

RICE IN LEGEND

Rice appears in many legends in Asia. In one Hindu myth from India, a beautiful woman agreed to marry the god Shiva if he could give her food she would never tire of. He couldn't find it and the woman died, but from her grave a new plant sprouted. Shiva collected the grains from the plant and gave rice to his people.

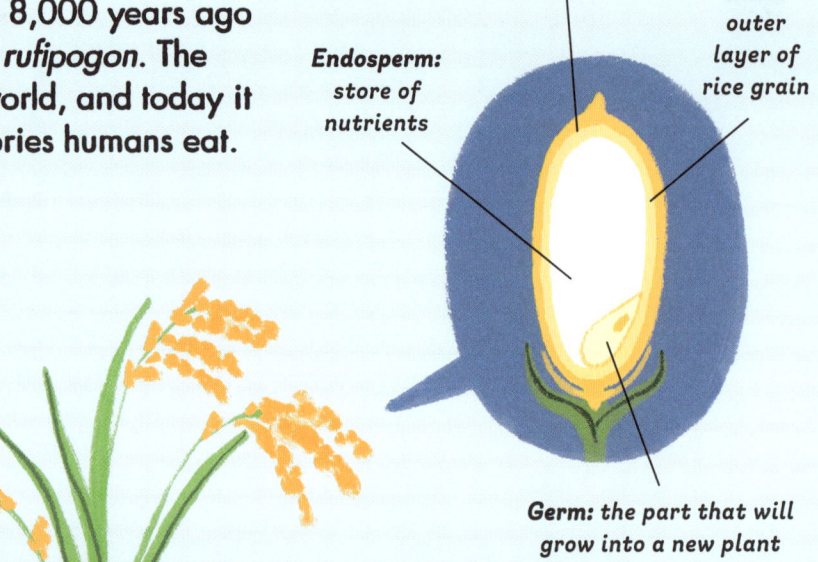

Hull: inedible outer layer

Bran: outer layer of rice grain

Endosperm: store of nutrients

Germ: the part that will grow into a new plant

TASTY SEEDS

We eat the kernels of the rice plant. Once rice is harvested, the hull is removed by a process known as threshing. This leaves the endosperm, which contains the germ, or embryo. Brown rice keeps its bran layer but this is removed from white rice.

Young rice needs lots of water, so it is grown in a purposely flooded 'paddy' field. Some paddy fields are irrigated from nearby rivers, while others are flooded during monsoons (heavy seasonal rain).

THE GREAT WALL OF RICE

When the Great Wall of China was built, it is said that *congee*, a sticky rice breakfast porridge, was added to the mortar. It was strong, waterproof and stopped weeds growing between the bricks.

Some rice varieties have been specially bred to have deeper-reaching roots. This helps the plant find nutrients and water in times of drought.

LET'S EAT WHEAT

Stone-Age humans gathered wild grasses more than 17,000 years ago, chewing the seeds raw or boiling them before eating. Around 10,000 years ago people began to cultivate wheat as a crop. Like rice, it provides around 15 per cent of the world's calories today.

WILD GRASS

Wheat began as a wild grass called einkorn, growing in the area around the Tigris and Euphrates river system near modern-day Iraq.

WHEAT IS EVERYWHERE!

Wheat is grown on nearly one-fifth of Earth's cultivated land. It is found in bread, pasta, noodles, cakes, breakfast cereal, biscuits, dumplings, puddings, pastry and many more types of food.

*Wheat contains a substance called **gluten**. Most people can eat gluten without problems, but some find it hard to digest. A few people suffer from coeliac disease, meaning they are allergic to gluten.*

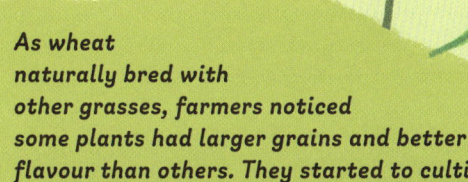

As wheat naturally bred with other grasses, farmers noticed some plants had larger grains and better flavour than others. They started to cultivate the grasses with the best flavours and biggest harvests.

OTHER GRAINS

More than half of the global population's food energy comes from corn, rice and wheat, but we eat hundreds of different kinds of grains and cereals.

Oats

Oats are often eaten ground or rolled as porridge.

Barley

Barley is the fourth most important grain crop after corn, rice and wheat.

Rye

Rye grain and flour is used in Northern and Eastern Europe.

Millet

Millet is a staple food across Africa and Asia.

Sorghum

Sorghum is the fifth most important cereal crop in the world and is valuable in hot, dry regions.

Spelt

Spelt was one of the first grains used to make bread.

AROUND THE WORLD: GRAINS AND CEREALS

From bread and cakes to pasta and countless cooked dishes, so many foods are made with cereals. Many are staple foods and people have found lots of delicious ways to use them.

Pancakes are flat cakes cooked in a frying pan.

MAKING BREAD

Bread is made with grains such as wheat, rye or spelt. The grain is ground into flour for the dough. Breads are leavened (made to rise with a raising agent, like yeast) or unleavened (flat).

Hundreds of cakes are made with wheat flour.

Croissants are crescent-shaped pastries, now associated with France. They actually originate from a bread first baked in seventeenth-century Austria to celebrate a military victory over the Ottoman Empire.

Pumpernickel is a dark rye bread from Germany.

The **Paris-Brest cake** is a wheel-shaped cake that was created to celebrate a bicycle race in France that started in 1891.

Naan is an oven-baked flatbread eaten mainly in Western Asia.

A traditional Australian soda bread or **damper** is cooked over a campfire.

Cornbread is a crumbly bread made from ground corn and cooked in a cast-iron pan, from the southern states of the USA.

Cornish pasties are filled with meat and potatoes. They were made for miners to take to work.

A baguette is a long stick of bread. They are bought daily in France so people can enjoy them at their freshest.

WHERE DID PASTA COME FROM?

Some people believe the Italian explorer Marco Polo brought noodles back from China. However, pasta may have developed separately, originating from the ancient Etruscan people of central Italy. Various forms of pasta and noodles are known in the ancient world across Europe, the Middle East and parts of Asia.

OODLES OF NOODLES

Noodles are made of soft wheat or rice flour, salt and sometimes egg, giving them a silky texture. They have been eaten in East Asia for thousands of years, and the world's oldest bowl of noodles, unearthed in China, dates back 4,000 years.

Ragù alla bolognese, known as spaghetti bolognese, is long pasta with meat sauce from the Italian city of Bologna.

In the Italian dish *lasagne*, thin, flat pasta is layered with meat or vegetable sauce.

Wontons are a style of Chinese dumpling made with various fillings. Sometimes they are served in broth with noodles.

Sombi is a sweet, coconut-flavoured rice pudding from Senegal.

Pad thai is a stir-fried rice noodle dish from Thailand.

Nasi goreng is Indonesian fried rice. It is often served with an egg, cucumber and tomato.

Chipa guasu is a savoury baked corn cake from Paraguay, made with corn, cheese and onion.

Gyoza are Japanese dumplings made with wheat dough wrappers and savoury fillings.

Ugali is a corn porridge eaten in sub-Saharan Africa.

Rice is cooked with meat and seafood in *paella*, a Spanish dish from Valencia.

MIGHTY MILK

All mammals, including humans, produce nutrient-rich milk to feed their babies. Over 200 million litres are consumed by humans every year and more than 85 per cent of it comes from cows. People have been drinking the milk of other animals for thousands of years, as well as turning it into a variety of foods, including cheese, yoghurt and butter.

Pasteurised milk is heated to a high temperature, then quickly cooled to kill dangerous bacteria.

YOGHURT

Milk can be turned into soft, creamy yoghurt. It is made by introducing a 'culture' made from millions of bacteria, which ferment (break down) the milk's lactose (sugars) into lactic acid. This makes the milk curdle, and it begins to sour and becomes slightly fizzy. People have eaten yoghurt in both sweet and savoury dishes for thousands of years.

Cream is a rich natural fat that rises to the top of milk. It is used to make food taste richer, to add thickness to sauces and soups... and, of course, to make ice cream!

Greek yoghurt is traditionally made from strained sheep's milk.

Dahi from India is thick and curd-like. It's usually made from cow's milk.

Skyr is an Icelandic sour-milk product, eaten like yoghurt.

THE MILK GENE

When we are babies we produce lactase, a substance that allows us to digest the lactose in milk. Most mammals stop making lactase as they grow older, but a gene in human DNA (the genetic code that makes up our bodies) that allows us to digest milk as adults can be found in Northern Europeans, East Africans and some other peoples with long histories of dairy farming. No one is sure why this genetic change happened, but some think it was the body's way of making up for the lack of vitamin D in countries without much sunlight.

DAIRY ANIMALS

Not all milk comes from cows. People have domesticated many 'dairy' animals that thrive in a variety of different conditions.

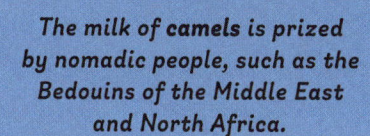

The milk of camels is prized by nomadic people, such as the Bedouins of the Middle East and North Africa.

Yaks are found in mountainous places, such as the Himalayas, Mongolia and parts of China. Every part of the yak is useful, especially its milk, which is rich and sweet because of the wildflowers they eat.

Goats are not fussy eaters, so they can survive where the land is tough. Fresh goats' milk has a sweet, earthy flavour.

Sheep are farmed for wool and milk. Yoghurt and cheese made from sheep's milk is especially popular in Southern Europe.

Found throughout Asia, **water buffalo** are used for ploughing and transport, as well as for their milk.

Zebu are a kind of cattle with humped shoulders, mainly found in Africa and India. Their milk takes on a nutty flavour when it is boiled.

For many northern communities in cold countries, such as Norway and Russia, the **reindeer** is the only animal that can be farmed. Their milk is very high in fat.

Cows are kept all over the world. Breeds in cold climates, like the Highland cow from Scotland, have developed tough, shaggy coats.

PLANT-BASED MILK

The Earth's climate is going through some serious changes and we are beginning to realise that too much dairy farming is not good for the environment (see pages 58–59). Plant-based alternatives, such as soya, oat and coconut milk, are becoming more and more popular.

THE STORY OF CHEESE

An Arabian legend tells how the first cheese was made by accident when a merchant travelled across the desert carrying some milk in a sheep's stomach. The sheep's stomach contained a substance called rennet, which made the milk curdle, turning it lumpy. The result – a soft cheese – was very tasty indeed!

ANCIENT CHEESE

This is a fun story, but we now know cheese goes back much earlier than the first Arabian merchants. Chinese mummies, 3,600 years old, have been found with lumps of cheese around their necks and archaeologists in Poland have found traces in pots that are more than 7,000 years old.

However cheese was invented, people realised that if the liquid was taken out of fresh milk, it would solidify and last much longer.

HOW CHEESE IS MADE

The simplest cheeses are made by straining milk in a cloth to leave soft 'curds'. Many cheeses are made using a more complex process, and a cheese's texture and flavour will vary according to how it was made.

1. Milk is gently heated with a 'starter culture' of bacteria and rennet.

2. The bacteria changes the lactose into lactic acid.

3. The milk 'curdles' (separates) into solids (curds) and liquid (whey).

4. The curds are drained from the whey, and salt is added.

5. The curds are put into moulds with salt and pressed to remove the rest of the whey.

6. The curds are left to mature (age) so they can slowly gain a stronger, more interesting flavour.

Depending on how long they are left to mature, cheeses can be fresh – soft and white – or hard. The harder the cheese, the less moisture it contains and the longer it will last.

CHEESES OF THE WORLD

Many regions take huge pride in their own special cheeses. There are many varieties.

Paneer is a soft Indian cheese made by curdling milk with acid from citrus fruits such as lemons.

Stilton can only be made in Derbyshire, Nottinghamshire or Leicestershire in England. It has blue 'veins', which are fungal cultures introduced to make the taste stronger.

Brie is a soft cheese from France, with a thick, white rind.

Tangy, crumbly and soft, **feta** is from Greece.

Parmesan is a hard Italian cheese that is often grated on top of pasta dishes.

A smooth Swiss cheese, **Emmental** is full of holes. They are made by carbon dioxide produced by bacteria when the curds are pressed.

Leipäjuusto is a fresh cheese from Finland, traditionally made with reindeer milk.

There is even sweet cheese! **Gjetost** is a fudge-like cheese from Norway.

Sherkam is a dried, smoked yak cheese eaten in the Eastern Himalayas.

Monterey Jack is a mild cheese from the United States.

Mish is a salty, fermented cheese spread from Egypt. It is thought to have been made there for over 5,000 years.

This Sardinian cheese, **casu marzu**, is allowed to mature outside, where flies lay their eggs on it. It is eaten with live maggots.

Milbenkäse, a German cheese, is matured by allowing bugs called mites to crawl over it. People love the taste of the cheese – and the mites!

Vieux-Boulogne is known as the world's smelliest cheese! It's even banned from public transport in France. Bacteria in the beer that is used to wash the rind react with the cheese to create the strong odour.

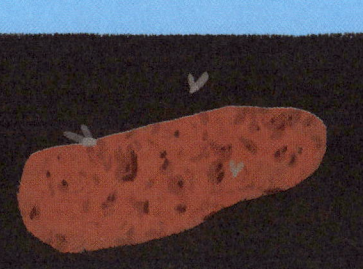

33

BUTTER

Rich and creamy, butter is an ancient – and delicious – way of preserving milk. It has been made for at least 4,000 years. In ancient times it was so popular with the Thracians, a people who lived north of Greece, that one Greek writer called them 'butter-eaters'.

MAKING BUTTER

Butter is made by churning cream, moving it constantly to separate out the fats from the liquid (buttermilk). After around 30 minutes of churning, the cream separates into butter and buttermilk.

Churning machine

Many stories of supernatural beings grew around butter. In Ireland, if the butter turned bad it was thought it had been tainted by fairies.

CHURNING

Traditionally, butter was churned by hand in a wooden container called a 'churn', which had a long pole in the middle that was moved up and down. It was backbreaking work, usually done by women – in fact the word 'dairy' comes from the old English term dæge, or 'female servant'. Today, butter is usually made in machines.

Butter is often eaten spread on bread or melted on top of vegetables, fish and meat. Some recipes also use butter as a fat for frying or as an ingredient in cakes and pastries.

Margarine is a butter substitute invented in 1869 by a French chemist when butter was scarce. To start with, it was made with beef fat, but today it is usually made with olive, sunflower and other plant oils.

Ghee is clarified butter used in Middle Eastern and Indian cooking, in both savoury dishes and sweets. Mysore pak is an Indian sweet made from ghee, sugar and gram flour, and is popular during the Hindu festival of Dussehra.

EGGS

Most creatures start life as eggs, which, if fertilised, can turn into young. Some animals, like mammals, keep their eggs inside them and give birth to live babies, while others, like birds, 'lay' eggs, which babies hatch from. Eggs eaten by humans are usually laid by birds, especially chickens.

LOTS OF EGGS

Humans eat more than one trillion chicken eggs every year. The eggs of other birds, including ducks, quails and geese, are also popular. The largest of all eggs – the enormous ostrich egg – makes a huge omelette!

Quail

Chicken

Duck

Goose

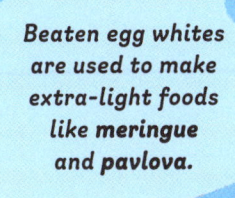

Ostrich

WHY CAN YOU BEAT AN EGG?

One of the many properties of eggs is that you can beat air into them to make a light and fluffy mixture. Egg whites contain protein, which forms a kind of skin around each bubble of air that you whisk into them. Soon, the whites swell up into a stiff foam. The fat in yolks prevents the skin forming around the bubbles, so whites and yolks are often prepared separately.

Beaten egg whites are used to make extra-light foods like meringue and pavlova.

WHEN IS AN EGG NOT AN EGG?

Most eggs are bought fresh in their shells, but they can also be bought as cans of just whites or just yolks or even dried into powder to make them easy to transport. People add water to the powder to use them in cooking. Today, vegan 'eggs' are also sold in some supermarkets.

Vegan eggs are made from plants and often come in powder form.

Powdered egg

Liquid egg yolks

Liquid egg whites

AROUND THE WORLD: DAIRY AND EGGS

Soufflé is a very light French dish made with beaten eggs and baked in the oven.

In England, boiled eggs wrapped in meat and deep fried are known as **Scotch eggs**.

The Swedish **gubbröra** is an open sandwich with egg and anchovies, served with dill.

Huevos rancheros is a Mexican breakfast dish of eggs, beans, rice, potatoes and tortillas.

Tamagoyaki is a type of Japanese omelette, where thin layers of cooked egg are rolled into a log shape and cut into slices.

Served in Norway, **Norsk eggekaffe** is coffee brewed with an egg. Some people have found that brewing coffee with an egg helps to filter it for a smoother taste.

Kwek kwek, a popular street food of quails' eggs coated in orange batter, fried and served with barbecue sauce, is eaten in the Philippines.

Obatzda from Germany is soft cheese mixed with butter and seasoned with spices.

Century eggs from China are duck eggs preserved in a special mixture for several months, which turns the yolks a green or grey colour.

The **khachapuri** from Georgia is a boat-shaped cheese pie, topped with an egg.

The **Spanish tortilla** is a thick omelette fried with potatoes, cooked in a pan on the stove top.

The Egyptian dish, **Baid mutajjan**, is hard-boiled eggs fried with spices.

Fondue from Switzerland is a large pot of melted cheese sauce that people dip bread and vegetables into.

Provoleta is a cheese from Argentina, most often served in discs that have been barbecued on a grill.

Strangolapreti are a type of gnocchi made with bread and spinach, served with a butter sauce.

Canadian **poutine** is a dish of fries served with cheese curds and gravy on top.

Butter chicken, from India, is a mild chicken and tomato curry dish, enriched with butter and cream.

In **eggs Benedict**, an American breakfast dish, an English muffin with ham and eggs is topped with creamy Hollandaise sauce.

Tzatziki is eaten in Southern Europe and the Middle East. This sauce is made with yoghurt, cucumber and fresh herbs.

ALL ABOUT MEAT

Our earliest ancestors were probably scavengers, eating meat from dead animals that they found. Eventually, humans developed tools and began to hunt for themselves. Rich in protein, meat is a large part of many diets today.

THE BIG FIVE
Today, most of the meat eaten around the globe comes from just five animals:

Goats can survive in places where cattle cannot live, such as mountains. They are not fussy about what they eat and some even climb trees!

HOW MUCH DO WE EAT?
Different parts of the world eat very different quantities of meat. People in the United States eat around 120 kilograms per person a year on average – the most in the world. In India, it's closer to 5 kilograms per person a year.

Pigs give us the most commonly eaten meat in the world. The meat of pigs is often 'cured' or preserved to make ham, bacon and sausages.

MEAT THE REST
Although millions depend on the 'big five', people also farm many other creatures for meat.

Rabbits were farmed by the ancient Romans in Spain, where they ran wild.

Alligator is eaten in the Southern United States. Grilled 'gator is a popular Cajun dish.

Native to the Americas, *turkey* is popular at festivals, including Thanksgiving and Christmas.

Guinea pigs are a type of rodent native to South America, where they are a popular food.

The modern chicken is descended from the red junglefowl of Southeast Asia. It was domesticated by humans, and archaeologists have found chicken bones in China dating back to around 5400 BCE.

Cows *have been bred for centuries for their milk, leather and meat. Spanish settlers brought cows to the United States, where they were herded on open ranges by gauchos and cowboys. Cows need a lot of grass to eat and 60 per cent of the world's farmland is taken up by cattle.*

Sheep *are able to nibble short grass, so can be farmed in places with poor soil. They are kept for both their meat and wool.*

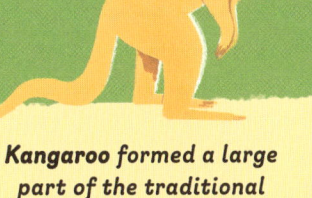

Kangaroo *formed a large part of the traditional diet of Australia's Indigenous people.*

Snails *are popular in Europe and West Africa. In France, escargots ('snails' in French) are cooked in their shells with garlic, butter and parsley.*

EATING INSECTS

In many countries, insects are a popular food and an important source of protein. Grasshoppers are eaten in places including Thailand, Mexico and Uganda, while silkworm pupae are a popular snack in China and Korea. In New Zealand, huhu grubs, the larvae of the huhu beetle, have been enjoyed for centuries by Māori people.

EXTREME CONDITIONS

In polar or mountainous regions hardy animals are an important part of people's diets. Alpacas have been farmed throughout South America for around 6,000 years, including high in the Andes mountains, while in the Himalayas people herd yaks for meat and milk.

MEAT-FREE DIETS

In many parts of the world throughout history, meat-eating was restricted to special occasions, except among the wealthy or elite. Today, many people avoid eating meat periodically or completely. This may be for religious reasons or because of concerns about animal welfare and the environment (see page 58).

FISH AND SEAFOOD

About 70 per cent of the Earth's surface is covered with water, so it's hardly surprising that we get a lot of our food from oceans, lakes and rivers. Life in the water is as varied as it is on land, and people around the world have learned which plants and creatures are good to eat.

HOW WE FISH

How fish are caught often affects whether they are sustainable or not. Sustainable fishing means damaging the environment as little as possible and leaving some fish to reproduce. Many countries have strict rules about the size of holes in fishing nets, so smaller, younger fish can escape.

Cod is one of the most popular fish in the world but it is often overfished.

Some 'trawler' boats drag giant nets across the seabed, scooping up everything, including creatures no one eats, which are wasted.

Shellfish like *clams* and *cockles* are usually harvested by hand.

Skipjack and *yellowfin* are types of tuna, often sold canned.

Sturgeon is often farmed for its meat and eggs, which are known as caviar.

Sole

Flounder

Lobsters are caught in cages called 'lobster pots'.

Coley, also known as pollack.

Crabs live on the seabed.

Monkfish are also known as anglerfish because they lure their prey with a 'rod' that grows on their head.

CLIMATE CHANGE

Climate change is affecting where fish live, and some waters are becoming too warm for species to survive. Many fish have also been affected by overfishing and pollution. Even medicines that have passed through our bodies and ended up in the sea can kill marine life.

FRESHWATER FISH

Fish also come from rivers and lakes. We call these freshwater fish.

With distinctive whisker-like 'barbels' around their mouths, **catfish** can be found in almost all parts of the world.

Tilapia are native to Africa, but, like salmon, are now farmed in many parts of the world.

Salmon famously swim upstream to spawn (lay eggs). Their flesh is pink or orange in colour.

FISHING SUSTAINABLY

The most sustainable forms of fishing involve catching one fish at a time – with a rod and line or a spear, for example. Buying tuna that was caught with a pole and line means that dolphins and other animals don't accidentally get caught in nets.

'Cast-net' fishing uses small nets to catch enough fish to sell in a market, without stripping the ocean of everything.

Herring is a silver fish, often eaten smoked or pickled. You'll find it in cans in the supermarket.

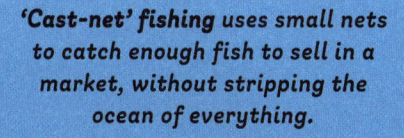

Eels are long, thin, snake-like fish.

Prawns and shrimps are small crustaceans – creatures with their skeletons on the outside of their bodies.

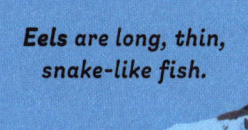

Octopuses have soft bodies and eight legs covered with suckers.

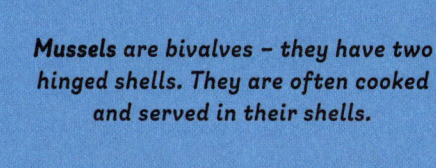

Mussels are bivalves – they have two hinged shells. They are often cooked and served in their shells.

AROUND THE WORLD: MEAT AND SEAFOOD

Humans have always roasted meat over open fires. Today, cooking meat, seafood and vegetables on a **barbecue** is common in many parts of the world.

In Argentina a barbecue is known as an **asado**, and is especially valued as a chance to socialise with friends and family.

Goulash is a Hungarian meat stew flavoured with paprika.

Haggis is a mix of minced meat, spices and herbs. This Scottish food is traditionally cooked in an animal's stomach.

Laulau are parcels of pork rolled in taro leaves, from Hawaii.

A rich fish and seafood soup, **bouillabaisse** comes from Marseilles, France.

Jerk is a famous Jamaican dish that uses a blend of spices and hot Scotch bonnet chillies.

Tourtière is a French-Canadian meat pie.

Beijing roast duck, also known as Peking duck, became associated with the Chinese imperial court in the Yuan dynasty around 700 years ago. Peking is the old name for Beijing.

In the UK, a **roast dinner** is traditionally eaten on Sundays when the family is together. Roast meat, often beef, lamb or pork, and vegetables are served with gravy (meat sauce).

Fish and chips is an English dish of white fish fried in batter with potato chips.

Frankfurters are sausages, originally made in Frankfurt, Germany. They were introduced to the United States in around 1900 and are now the key ingredient in American hot dogs.

In New Zealand, a **hāngi** is a traditional Māori cooking method where meat and vegetables are cooked in an underground oven.

In the Japanese cooking technique known as **teriyaki**, a variety of meat and fish are marinated in soy sauce.

Moules-frites is a dish of mussels and French fries from Belgium.

Koftas are spicy, herby meatballs, eaten in the Middle East, North Africa, Central Asia, India, Greece and the Balkans.

In Japan, thinly sliced raw fish is known as **sashimi**.

Gumbo is a spicy fish, seafood or meat stew from the Southern United States.

In Iceland, fish is hung in the frozen air to dry, then pounded into thin sheets known as **harðfiskur**. The preserved strips are eaten with butter.

Spiced, dried strips of meat from Southern Africa are known as **biltong**. Because meat was 'cured' (preserved) with salt it could be taken on long journeys.

Ceviche is the national dish of Peru. It is raw fish prepared in the acid from lime juice.

Chilli con carne, a dish of minced meat cooked with chilli peppers, is a Mexican-American dish that was probably invented in Texas, where it's the state dish.

Canh chua is a Vietnamese sour and spicy fish soup enjoyed cold during the summer.

Hamburgers are so-called in the United States because they originated from the German 'Hamburg steak', a type of meat patty. They came to the United States with German migrants and gradually extras have been added, such as the bun, pickles, sauces and slices of cheese.

SALT

Salt is the mineral sodium chloride. It is usually either mined from the earth as 'rock salt' or harvested from saline (salty) water as 'sea salt'.

OUR BODIES NEED SALT

The salt in our bodies helps to maintain fluid levels and keep the heart, liver and kidneys healthy. Too little salt and we can't function: we become tired, we might lose consciousness and, in extreme instances, even die.

We lose salt every time we sweat (this is why your sweat tastes salty), so we constantly need to replace it.

MAKING FOOD LAST

Before refrigeration, our ancestors realised that fish and meat could be preserved in salt to make it last the winter or on long sea voyages.

*In Norway, salted, dried fish is known as **klippfisk** (meaning 'cliff fish'), because it is traditionally salted on the cliffs near the sea.*

NOT TOO MUCH

Some manufacturers have added more salt than they should to processed foods to make them tasty. Too much salt has been associated with high blood pressure, bone problems, kidney disease and even cancer.

PEPPER

Pepper comes from the fruits of a flowering vine. The berries, which have a thin skin and a large seed, are dried, then ground to use as a spice.

A VALUABLE TRADE

Pepper originated in Kerala, India, and is thought to be one of the earliest spices traded – traces have been found in ancient Egyptian tombs.

*In medieval times, **pepper** was so valuable that traders told their customers that serpents guarded the pits where it was kept to keep the prices high.*

STAR SPICE

Pepper is now one of the most popular spices in the world, used in nearly every cuisine. The biggest producer is Vietnam, which grows around one-third of the world's supply.

*The pungent 'bite' of pepper comes from a substance called **piperine**.*

*Most pepper dishes are savoury. Nigerian **catfish pepper soup** uses it to spice the fish without overwhelming its delicate flavour.*

44

HOT, HOT CHILLIES

Chilli peppers add heat and spice to food. They are fruits, and members of the plant family that contains tomatoes, potatoes and sweet peppers. It is believed that people have been growing and trading chillies for more than 6,000 years.

SPICY HEAT

The spicy heat of chilli comes from capsaicin, a chemical in the pith (spongy white flesh) that surrounds the seeds, not the seeds themselves.

Chillies come from South America. Europeans were first introduced to the hot peppers in the sixteenth century and they took some home with them.

Once chillies had arrived in Europe, it didn't take long for them to become popular across the world. India is now one of the world's largest producers.

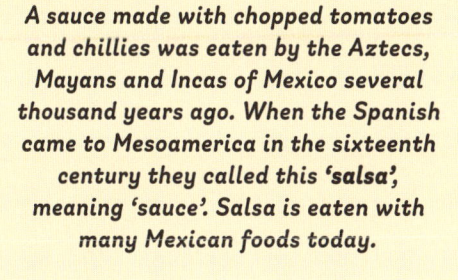

A sauce made with chopped tomatoes and chillies was eaten by the Aztecs, Mayans and Incas of Mexico several thousand years ago. When the Spanish came to Mesoamerica in the sixteenth century they called this **'salsa'**, meaning 'sauce'. Salsa is eaten with many Mexican foods today.

Phall is a British-Indian tomato-based dish, and one of the hottest curries you can buy!

Phall is made with up to 10 or 12 **habanero peppers**. Some restaurants in Birmingham, UK, offer customers special prizes if they can finish the dish!

THE CHILLI PEPPER SCALE

There are more than 400 varieties of chilli, all with different strengths of heat. In 1912, Wilbur Scoville developed the Scoville Test to measure out how hot a chilli is. Chilli heat is now graded in Scoville Heat Units (SHU).

Ají dulce
Mild 0–1000 SHU

Bishop's crown
5,000–30,000 SHU

Habanero
100,000–350,000 SHU

Carolina reaper
The world's hottest chilli!
1,400,000–2,200,000 SHU

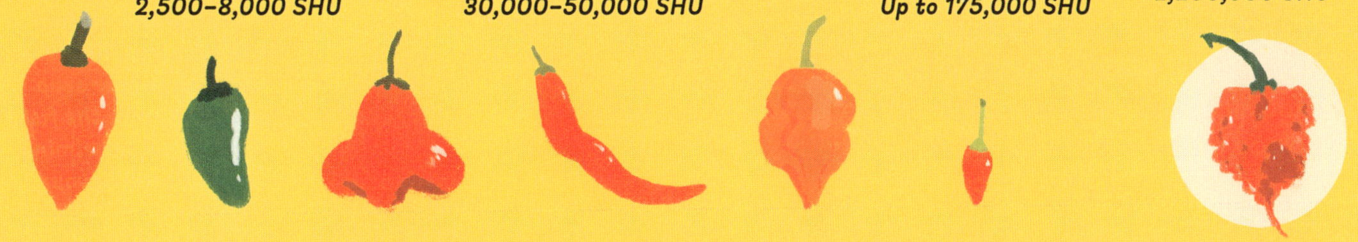

Jalapeño
2,500–8,000 SHU

Cayenne
30,000–50,000 SHU

African bird's eye
Up to 175,000 SHU

HERBS AND SPICES

Many plants have strong, distinctive flavours, colours or smells. Depending on the plant, we use roots, bark, stems, leaves, flowers and fruits to make food taste exciting. Generally, herbs are the green, leafy parts of plants, while spices tend to be the drier, harder parts, such as roots, seeds, stems or bark.

Harissa is a hot paste made from chilli and a blend of spices such as coriander, cumin and caraway seeds, used in Tunisian cuisine.

Vanilla is a spice that comes from the seed pod of an orchid. It was possibly first used by the Olmec people of Mexico.

The aromatic spice *star anise* comes from the star-shaped seed pods of a member of the Magnolia family.

A hot, spicy root, *horseradish* is in the Brassica family, which also includes mustard and wasabi. It accompanies foods in many cuisines, including steak, fish and eggs.

Like horseradish, *wasabi* is a hot, spicy root, and it is eaten as a paste in Japanese cuisine.

Ginger is a rhizome, a kind of root, with a hot, fresh flavour.

Chives are a tiny member of the onion family that are harvested for their tasty long, thin leaves.

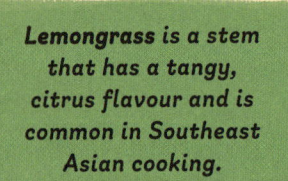

Lemongrass is a stem that has a tangy, citrus flavour and is common in Southeast Asian cooking.

As well as adding aromatic flavour in food, *cloves* have been used for centuries to soothe toothache.

Once one of the world's most expensive spices, *nutmeg* is still highly valued.

Pungent and bright red, *saffron* comes from the stamens of the saffron crocus flower. It takes around 150,000 flowers to make one kilo of saffron.

Turmeric comes from a root that is a member of the ginger family. It is important in Southeast Asia for its flavour and yellow colour.

Paprika is a red spice made from ground, dried peppers. It is a key ingredient in Spanish paella (see page 29).

Cinnamon is the inner bark of cinnamon trees, which are native to Sri Lanka. It has been used as a spice since ancient times.

In France, herbs such as parsley, thyme and bay are sometimes tied together in a bunch called a **bouquet garni**. It's added to dishes such as soups and stews to add flavour during cooking but is removed before serving.

The **curry tree** is native to India and it's actually a member of the citrus family. Its leaves are used in sauces and to flavour rice in India and several Southeast Asian countries.

The Ancient Romans thought the herb **thyme** protected the eater from poisoning.

Mustard seeds are ground into a sauce that is used as a condiment in many countries.

The aromatic seed pods of **cardamom** are used in Middle Eastern sweets and spices and in many Indian dishes.

Cumin seeds are used in Latin American, Middle Eastern and Indian cuisines. Often toasted, they add a warm, earthy flavour.

Basil is a popular herb, especially in Italian dishes. It is one of the main ingredients of pesto sauce.

There are 25 species of **mint**, all slightly different. Mint sauce is a condiment for roast lamb in Britain.

Parsley is used in many dishes, such as in tabbouleh, a Lebanese salad.

Coriander can be used as both a herb and a spice. We chop the leaves and stems into dishes and grind the dried seeds into a spice.

47

HONEY

Honey is made by bees to feed their young, but animals — and humans — began to eat it thousands of years ago. For centuries it was one of our only sources of sweetness, so it has always been highly prized.

An 8,000-year-old cave painting in Spain shows someone climbing a tree to collect wild honey.

The first beekeeping we know about was in Tel Rehov, Israel, around 1,000 years ago. Archaeologists have discovered clay cylinders built for bees to live in.

HOW HONEY IS MADE

It takes about 12 bees their entire lifetimes to make a teaspoon of honey.

1. Bees visit flowers to harvest a sweet juice called nectar. They suck it out with long tongues.

2. Bees store nectar in a special 'honey stomach' (different from their food stomach), as they fly from flower to flower.

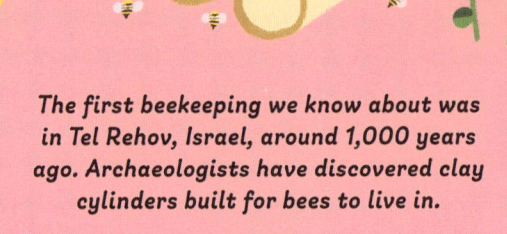

3. Back at the hive, worker bees transfer the nectar from returning bees to house bees. The house bees' job is to chew the nectar until it turns into a syrup — honey. They then seal the honey inside hexagonal cells made from wax until it's needed to feed young.

4. When humans harvest honey, they take some, leaving enough for the hive to live on.

WE NEED BEES

Around the world, there are fewer honeybees than there used to be. This may be due to the use of pesticides and herbicides, habitat loss, mites, diseases, climate change or a combination of all of these. Bees are vital, not just for honey, but as pollinators for food crops, so scientists are treating the problem very seriously.

Baklava is made from layers of thin pastry sheets and nuts, drenched in honey. It is a traditional sweet across Greece, the Balkans and the Middle East.

48

SUGAR

Everyone knows that chocolate, sweets, doughnuts and fizzy drinks contain sugar. But what about pasta sauces, baked beans and ketchup? If foods have been made in a factory, the chances are they contain sugar too. Sugar is sweet and delicious, so, often, we just can't resist it.

CANE AND BEET

Sugar cane is a tropical grass, with extremely sweet-tasting stems. Sugar beet is a root vegetable that grows easily in cooler countries. Both can be refined into sugar.

Sugar cane

Sugar beet

Lots of us have a 'sweet tooth'. This may be thanks to our primate ancestors, who needed carbohydrates in the form of sugars to make energy. Even today, our relations, the apes, always seek out the ripest fruits, with the highest sugar content.

NOT TOO SWEET

Sugar provides energy but very little other nutrition. A little bit of sweetness is very enjoyable, but we should be careful not to eat too much. Over time, eating too much sugar can cause us to gain weight and may increase risk of heart problems and diseases such as diabetes.

HOW SUGAR IS MADE

In a factory, sugar cane goes through many stages in order to become sugar.

1. Sugar cane is crushed to extract the juice.
2. The juice is boiled until it crystallises.
3. The crystals are spun in a machine called a centrifuge to remove the last of the liquid.
4. The sugar is dried and packaged.

SWEETNESS: THE HUMAN COST

Arabians introduced Europeans to sugar more than 1,000 years ago, and by the 1500s, they were producing it themselves. Harvesting the sugar cane was hard work, so the unscrupulous Europeans took captives from Africa and South America, and forced them to work on plantations in the West Indies and North America. Over the next 300 years, sugar became cheap and slave owners became wealthy. From the 1770s, there was a long struggle to abolish slavery. Enslaved people organised rebellions and played a key role in the passing of the Abolition of the Slave Trade Act in Britain in 1807. However, enslaved people in the British colonies were not emancipated (officially allowed freedom) until 1838. In the United States, slavery was abolished in 1865.

CHOCOLATE

Chocolate comes from the fruit of the *Theobroma cacao* tree from South America. Theobroma means 'food of the gods' in Greek. The seeds of the cacao tree, known as 'cocoa beans', grow inside a brightly coloured pod, which contains between 20 and 60 'beans', surrounded by pulp. About half of each bean is fat, which is called cocoa butter.

ANCIENT CHOCOLATE

We get the modern-day word 'chocolate' from *xocolatl*, the Aztec word for 'bitter water'. Archaeologists have found traces of cacao in Mesoamerican civilisations, as far back as 1400 BCE when it was probably grown by the Olmec people. Some even claim they have found evidence of chocolate up to 4,000 years ago!

Aztecs ground the cacao beans into a bitter drink. Royalty and priests drank chocolate at special ceremonies and warriors drank it before a battle for strength and stamina.

A SPOONFUL OF CHOCOLATE

Some people say Spanish conquistador Hernán Cortés brought cacao from South America back to Europe as a potential medicine. Physicians added sugar to it and the new wonder drug was found to miraculously help patients gain weight! The Spanish kept the recipe for chocolate closely guarded for a long time. But in the 1600s it was introduced to France by Anne, the daughter of King Philip III of Spain, and from there it became popular in other parts of Europe.

DELICIOSO!

CHOCOLATE BARS

The Industrial Revolution (mid 1700s–early 1900s) brought new processes that allowed chocolate to be produced in large quantities. More people could buy chocolate as a treat. Solid chocolate was invented in 1847 by Joseph Fry of England, but the first chocolate bars were gritty in texture.

HOW CHOCOLATE IS MADE

More than two-thirds of the world's cacao is grown in Africa. The Côte d'Ivoire grows around one-third of the world's supply. Cacao seeds have a very bitter taste and must be processed to achieve the texture and delicious flavour we recognise as chocolate. Cacao trees are usually grown on small farms by farmers, who often work together in cooperatives to get better trading prices. The pods are harvested twice a year.

1. The seed pods are harvested.

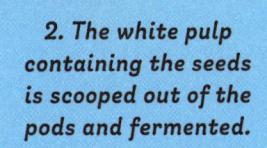

2. The white pulp containing the seeds is scooped out of the pods and fermented.

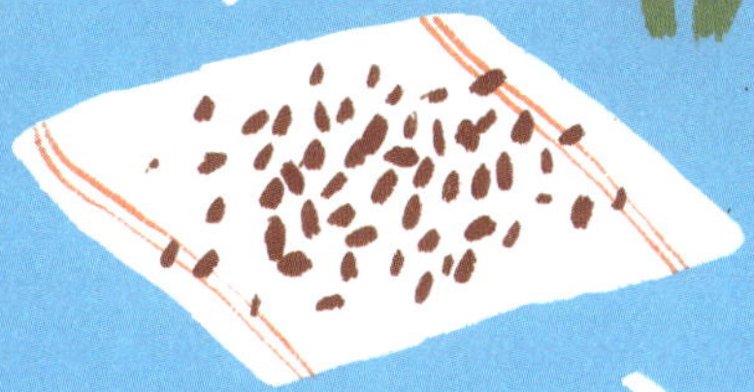

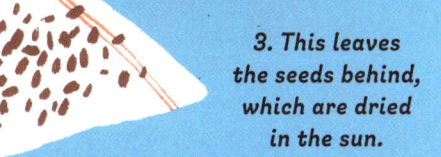

3. This leaves the seeds behind, which are dried in the sun.

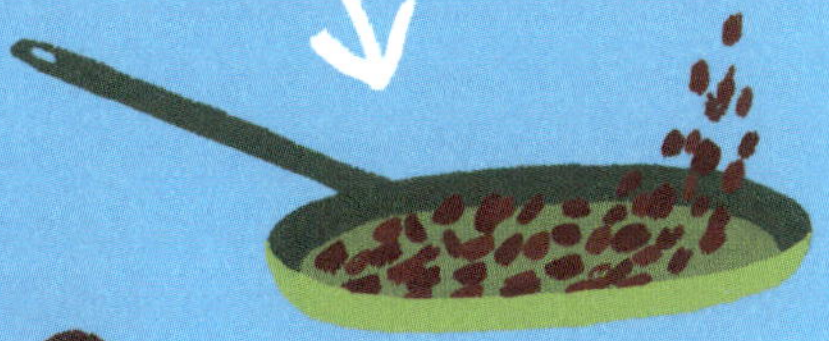

4. The cacao beans are roasted and the shells are cracked away. A small extract of each bean called a 'cacao nib' remains.

5. The nibs are turned into a paste with sugar and milk.

6. The paste is tempered (melted at an exact temperature and cooled) and moulded.

HOW WE EAT CHOCOLATE

Chocolate appears in all sorts of food. Many of them are sweet… but not all!

Chocolate cake

Brigadeiros

These chocolate fudge balls are popular in Brazil.

Chocolate ice cream

Chilli con carne

Recently, more people have rediscovered the ancient use of chocolate as a savoury spice. Some chefs add dark chocolate to **chilli con carne** to bring out other flavours.

AROUND THE WORLD: SWEETS

The Victoria sandwich from England has two sponge cakes with cream and jam in the middle.

Deep-fried Peruvian doughnuts, **picarones** are made from sweet potato and squash.

Dragon's beard candy is a white Chinese dessert made of spun sugar with a filling of peanuts, coconut or chocolate.

Gulab jamun are ball-shaped deep-fried sweets from India, served in syrup.

The Swedish layered sponge cake **prinsesstårta**, or 'princess cake', is finished with a layer of green marzipan and often a pink marzipan rose.

Tarte au citron is a tangy lemon tart from France.

Not all sweet things come from honey or sugar. **Maple syrup** is made from the sap of maple trees. In Canada and the United States it is especially popular on pancakes.

The popular Russian dessert **syrniki** are pancakes made with quark, a sour cream cheese.

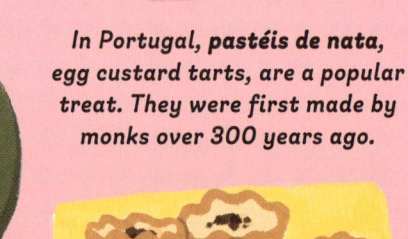

In Portugal, **pastéis de nata**, egg custard tarts, are a popular treat. They were first made by monks over 300 years ago.

Canadian **Nanaimo bars** have custard and melted chocolate on a biscuit base. They are named after the city of Nanaimo in British Colombia.

Soft and chewy, **mochi** are sweet rice paste balls from Japan.

Apfelstrudel, an Austrian rolled pastry, has an apple and raisin filling.

Lokum, also known as Turkish delight after their country of origin, are sweet jelly cubes often flavoured with rose water or lemon.

From Sicily in Italy, **cannoli** have a creamy cheese filling in a crisp, sweet shell.

Brownies are fudgy chocolate cakes from the United States.

Sweet, seashell-shaped buns called **conchas** are sold at bakeries throughout Mexico.

Crunchy and covered in sugar, **churros** are Spanish deep-fried dough sticks, often served with chocolate sauce.

Boortsog are deep-fried buttery biscuits from Mongolia.

Made with sugar, bananas and flour and served with coconut cream, **po'e** is a fruit pudding from Tahiti, in the South Pacific.

Tub tim krob from Thailand is an iced dessert with 'rubies' made from water chestnuts soaked in grenadine syrup and served in coconut milk.

A caramelised candy made with peanuts and coconut, **kashata** is from East Africa.

Esterházy torta is a layered cake from Hungary that has distinctive icing in a 'spider web' design.

Pavlova is a lightly baked soft meringue dessert named for the Russian ballerina Anna Pavlova, who toured Australia and New Zealand in the 1920s. Whipped cream and fresh fruit are often on top.

53

FESTIVE FOODS

Every community has special occasions, and preparing and sharing food is often a very important part of the festivities. Details may change and traditions may vary, but there are common themes of commemoration and celebration.

THE CHRISTMAS TABLE

Christmas is a Christian festival that celebrates the birth of Jesus. It is celebrated on various days in December and January in different communities, and food plays an important role.

It's thought that King Henry VIII was the first person to eat a *'Christmas turkey'* in England when it arrived in the 1520s from its native North and South America. It quickly became the popular centrepiece of the Christmas dinner and it's still eaten by many today.

Christmas pudding is a steamed fruit pudding eaten in the UK. It is often covered in brandy or whisky and set alight before being dished up!

In Germany, beautifully decorated *gingerbread houses* are made out of baked lebkuchen (gingerbread) biscuits.

A thick nougat candy from Spain, *turrón* is made with honey, sugar and egg whites.

Eaten in the Ukraine, *kutya* is a sweet porridge made of wheat grains mixed with seeds, honey and raisins.

From France, *Bûche de Noël* is a rolled chocolate cake decorated like a yule log. These were specially chosen logs burned in the home fire at Christmas in the Middle Ages.

A banquet of seven different fish and seafood dishes known as *the Feast of the Seven Fishes* is often eaten by Italian-American families on Christmas Eve.

Hallacas are corn dough stuffed with meat, vegetables or fruit, wrapped in banana leaves and boiled. They are eaten in Venezuela at Christmas.

Doro wat is a chicken stew from Ethiopia. At Christmas, a cockerel, instead of a chicken, is used. It's divided into 12 pieces representing the 12 disciples of Jesus.

THE DIWALI TABLE

Diwali is a festival of lights celebrated in November by many Hindus, Sikhs and Jains around the world. As well as sparking millions of candles and electric lights, people eat special food for several days. Diwali feasts are most famous for their *mithai* or sweets.

Barfi are fudge-like sweets made with condensed milk and sugar. They can be flavoured with pistachio, saffron and mango, and are often given as gifts during Diwali.

From India's Maharashtra region, *karanji* are crispy, fried, sweet-savoury pastries stuffed with coconut.

Mawa kachori, sweet pastries from Rajasthan, India, are stuffed with dried fruit and coated in sugar syrup.

Kheer is a rice pudding made with cardamom, raisins, almonds and saffron.

Halwa, grains or grated vegetables cooked with ghee, sugar, condensed milk and nuts, is a dish that came to India from the Middle East more than 500 years ago.

THE PASSOVER TABLE

Passover is an eight-day festival celebrated by Jewish people in early spring to commemorate the Israelites' release from captivity in Egypt. Anything involving *chametz* (leavened food) is avoided. The Seder is a feast observed on the first two nights of Passover with ceremonial food on a special plate called a *Ka'arah*.

Four cups of **wine** or grape juice celebrate freedom.

The **beitzah** is a roasted egg that represents temple sacrifices and the cycle of life.

Flat, unleavened bread called **matzah** is eaten to remember that when the Israelites left Egypt they did not have time for yeast to rise.

Maror is a bitter herb, often horseradish, that is eaten to remember the bitterness of slavery.

Karpas is a green vegetable, often parsley, which symbolises springtime and new beginnings. It is dipped in salt water, representing the tears of slavery.

KA'ARAH PLATE

Chazeret is a second bitter herb, usually a green one, that is also eaten.

Charoset is a sweet fruit paste which symbolises the mortar the Israelite slaves had to use.

Z'roa, the roasted shank bone of a lamb, stands for the lamb sacrificed at the first Passover.

THE EID TABLE

Eid al-Fitr is a special feast that marks the end of the Islamic holy month of Ramadan. In Ramadan, people fast during daylight hours for a month, so Eid al-Fitr is a celebration of food.

Tagine is a dish from North Africa of slow-cooked meat and vegetables. It is named after the special clay pot it is cooked in.

Sheer khurma, a vermicelli (thin noodles) milk pudding with pistachios and dried dates, is served in India, Afghanistan and Central Asia.

Common throughout the Middle East and Central Asia, *kebabs* are grilled meat skewers served with salad or eaten as they are.

Beef rendang is a spicy beef and coconut curry from Malaysia.

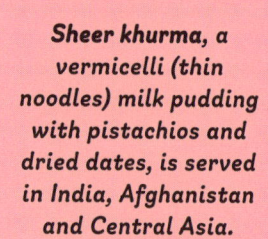

Cambaabur is a spiced Somali flatbread served with yoghurt and sugar.

Haleem is a slow cooked meat and lentil stew that came to India from Arabia during the Mughal Empire in the sixteenth century.

The 'thousand layers' cake, *lapis legit*, is eaten in Indonesia.

Traditional Lebanese buttery pastries, *ma'amoul* are often stuffed with dates.

A spicy rice dish with meat and vegetables, *biryani* is thought to have come to India from Persia.

THE THANKSGIVING TABLE

Thanksgiving is a holiday in November in North America to give thanks for blessings. Dishes served vary by region and family, but often include turkey, sweet potatoes and other foods native to the Americas. The holiday has its roots in the 1600s, when European settlers landed in North America, in Plymouth, Massachusetts.

Turkey is so important that the festival is sometimes known as Turkey Day. Turkeys are usually cooked with stuffing, a mixture of breadcrumbs, onions and sausage meat, inside. In California, this might be made with sourdough bread, while in the Midwest – especially Minnesota – a wild rice casserole is sometimes used. Turkey is often roasted with potato and sweet potato and served with cranberry sauce.

Cornbread is made with cornmeal (ground corn). At the first Thanksgiving corn was probably made into a kind of porridge.

THE CHINESE NEW YEAR TABLE

Chinese New Year celebrates the beginning of the new lunar year. It starts at the new moon that appears between 21 January and 20 February, and lasts for two weeks, until the full moon. The food eaten is selected to bring luck, happiness, money and health.

Fish represents prosperity, as the Chinese word for fish, "yu", sounds like the word for "abundance". Carp and catfish are both popular.

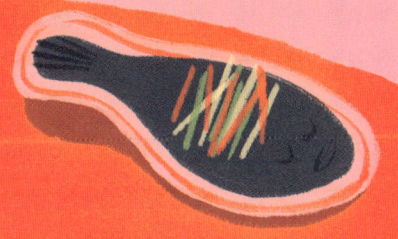

The round shape of **tangyuan**, sweet rice balls, represents a family gathering together.

Spring rolls, deep-fried filled pancakes, represent wealth because they look like gold bars.

Nian gao or 'New Year cakes' are sticky rice cakes that symbolise the promise of the New Year.

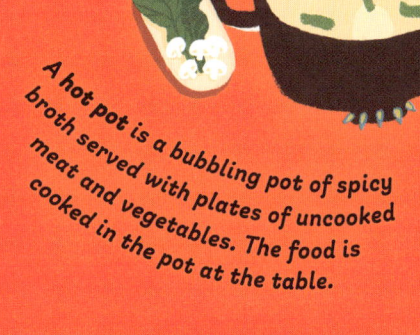

A **hot pot** is a bubbling pot of spicy broth, served with plates of uncooked meat and vegetables. The food is cooked in the pot at the table.

In Cantonese, a language from Southeastern China, the word for **lobster** means 'big dragon prawn', and like dragons, red lobsters are thought to bring luck.

Dumplings stuffed with minced meat, fish and vegetables are made in the shape of Chinese silver ingots to bring wealth.

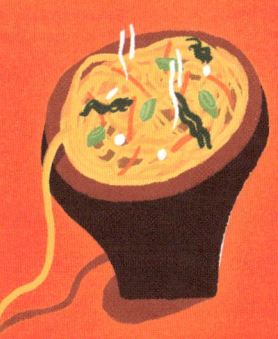

Longevity noodles are especially long, and are eaten for long life and happiness.

Sweet **pumpkin pie** was not served at the very first Thanksgiving dinner, but pumpkin would have appeared in some form.

Chitterlings are made from pig intestines and are part of the festive tradition in the Southern United States.

Manicotti are pasta tubes stuffed with ricotta cheese. Many Italian-American families might eat pasta before their turkey.

Green bean casserole is a favourite Midwestern dish that was invented in the 1950s to promote canned mushroom soup, which goes into the recipe!

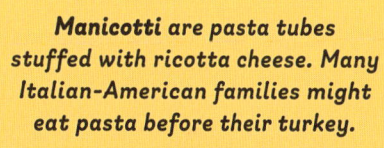

THE TRICKY QUESTIONS

Scientists estimate there will be nearly 10 billion people on Earth by 2050. This will put a lot more stress on our planet's resources. The world is facing a number of complicated environmental, social and economic problems caused by how we produce food and what we eat.

GREENHOUSE GASES

Since the 1960s the quantity of meat the world's population eats each year has gone from around 70 million tonnes to over 300 million tonnes. This means that there are billions more farm animals in the world. Cows, sheep and goats are 'ruminant' animals, which rely on microbes in their stomachs to break down the plants they eat. This creates methane, a 'greenhouse gas', which contributes to global warming. In addition, if food has to be transported a long distance before it is eaten, carbon dioxide, another greenhouse gas, is emitted into the air.

LOSING FORESTS

When they're kept well, animals take up a lot of land, which often means forests have been cut down. In the Amazon Rainforest 80 per cent of deforestation is to make way for cattle farms. But becoming vegetarian (not eating meat) isn't always straightforward either. In Southeast Asia and other places, rainforests are cut down to make room for single crops, such as palm oil trees, threatening species such as orangutans. As trees absorb carbon dioxide, a greenhouse gas, and release oxygen, the loss of forests contributes to climate change.

ANIMAL WELFARE

With a growing population, farming intensively (with animals very close together) has become common. This can be very cruel, and battery hens, for example, are kept in very small cages to produce eggs. 'Free range' eggs come from chickens that are free to explore their environments.

SHARING IT OUT

Around the world today, more than 800 million people do not have enough to eat. This is not because we do not produce enough food, but because it is not distributed evenly. Around a third of all food is lost or wasted.

BIODIVERSITY

Biodiversity (the diversity of wildlife) shrinks as plants and animals lose their habitats. This poses some enormous challenges to feeding the planet. Pesticides used in farming are killing bees, which pollinate crops, and other pollinators, such as bats and birds. In the oceans, pollution and climate change are endangering many species, including marine microorganisms like phytoplankton, which are the basis of the marine food chain. If they are disrupted, all other marine life will be too.

PLASTIC

Plastic can take hundreds of years to break down naturally. Often, food and drink are packaged in plastic, and up to half of all plastic items are used only once before they are thrown away. There may be as many as five trillion pieces of plastic in our oceans. Plastic particles in the environment are harmful to people and animals.

THE FUTURE OF FOOD

To make sure everybody has enough to eat, we need to think hard about what food to grow and how best to provide it. All over the world scientists and environmentalists are looking at how we can make sure food – and humans – have a bright future.

SUSTAINABILITY

Sustainability means living without depleting the natural resources of the planet. Sustainably produced food is farmed or gathered without destroying natural environments or causing animals to become extinct.

NEW INNOVATIONS

Technology is a vital tool in our quest to feed everyone without harming the environment. In the future we may even be able to eat using personalised nutrition plans according to our individual DNA!

Genetic engineering (editing or changing parts of DNA) can add nutrients to plants or subtly change them so they grow and taste better. For example, scientists have created a banana containing a vitamin the fruit doesn't normally have. This means that communities which rely on bananas can have a more nutritious diet.

New packaging made from materials such as corn starch and seaweed can either be eaten or will break down harmlessly into the soil instead of polluting the world's oceans like plastic does.

MORE VARIETY

We currently rely on a very small variety of foods – around 60 per cent of our food comes from just 12 plant and 5 animal species. This makes our food supply vulnerable to disease and climate change. If we eat more types of food we can ensure a more durable food supply. The following are already eaten in many places, but may be eaten more widely in the near future:

Seaweed is enjoyed in many cuisines, mainly in Asia.

*Ancient grains such as **spelt**, **bulgar**, **millet** and **quinoa** are often healthier than refined wheat flour.*

Cacti have been part of the Mexican diet for centuries.

*There are over 2,000 edible **fungi**, though we currently only eat around 350 varieties.*

Insects and grubs are a staple for many people of the world. Locusts, especially, are high in protein and are often made into flour.

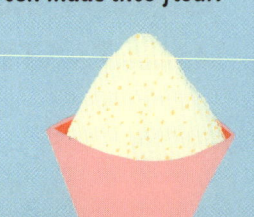

PLANT-BASED DIETS

An increasing number of people do not eat meat because of concerns about the welfare of animals and the environment. Alternatives such as tofu, made from soy beans, have been around for centuries, but there are also newer substitutes that look, taste, feel and cook exactly like meat, yet still come entirely from plants.

Algae produce oxygen and are full of protein, making them a possible substitute for meat. They also grow abundantly in comparatively small spaces, so can be produced more sustainably than many other foods.

PLANT-BASED DIETS

Many people are looking at ways to reduce food waste. The grain that breweries have finished with can be made into snack bars, and beer can even be brewed from old bread. Some fruit and vegetables are rejected by supermarkets because they are 'ugly', but some companies are now turning these into juice or soup.

OUR FOOD FUTURE

What and how we eat has changed constantly over the centuries and it is still changing today. By exploring the food people enjoy around the world and combining it with new technology, we can not only find new ways of keeping everyone healthy and well-fed, we can discover new flavours and experiences.

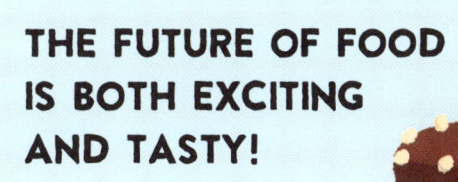

THE FUTURE OF FOOD IS BOTH EXCITING AND TASTY!

WHAT CAN I DO?

Governments and big businesses around the world need to work together to solve many of the problems with our food supply but there are smaller ways you can make a difference:

✓ *Check food labels to see that food has been farmed responsibly.*

✓ *Choose food that has been produced locally and hasn't been flown thousands of miles around the world.*

✓ *Eat protein sources like beans and tofu that have a lower carbon footprint.*

✓ *Grow your own food! Some vegetables and greens will even grow in pots on a window ledge.*

GLOSSARY

ANCIENT MESOPOTAMIA
An area of Western Asia, near Turkey, thought to be the place where humans first formed civilisations.

AROMATIC
To describe something that has a strong and pleasant smell, often fragrant or spicy.

BIOFUEL
A fuel that is made from plant material, animal waste and even algae.

BOTANY
The study of plants.

BRASSICAS
Members of the cabbage family, they are often but not always green and leafy.

BROMELIAD
A type of plant that mainly grows in tropical regions. The pineapple is one of only two edible bromeliads. The other is *Bromelia*, which has berries but is not widely eaten.

BROTH
A savoury liquid, made from water boiled with various ingredients for nutrition and flavour.

CAJUN
Someone from Louisiana, USA, with French-Canadian ancestry. This word also describes the cuisine from the same place.

CANOLA
A type of brassica whose seed is often used for oil.

CEREAL
Plants belonging to the grass family, which often produce grain.

CLIMATE CHANGE
The gradual change in average weather conditions over time. Human activities, which release greenhouse gases, have made the Earth's climate change quicker than normal.

CONDIMENT
A sauce or seasoning that is used to add flavour to food such as salt, ketchup or chilli flakes.

CONQUISTADORS
Spanish and Portuguese explorer-soldiers from the 1400s to the 1600s. Conquistadors invaded rather than traded with countries, mainly in South and Central America.

COOPERATIVE
A group of individuals, such as farmers, who work together voluntarily. By putting their resources together into one big pot, everyone can benefit from better prices for their goods and profits are shared evenly.

CROP
A plant that is grown or farmed for use by humans.

CUISINE
A style of cooking, usually used to describe the cooking of a country or region.

CULTIVATED
Land prepared for farming.

CULTURE
1) The way people live.
2) A mass of bacteria used to create some foods, such as yeasts, yoghurts and cheeses.

DOMESTICATE
To tame an animal as a pet or for farming.

FRUCTOSE
A sugar found in fruit.

FRUIT
The parts of a plant that contain its seeds.

GRAIN
Seeds, usually of grasses but sometimes of the legume or pea family, that have been harvested for human consumption.

GRAM
1) A metric unit of weight.
2) A type of flour made from ground chickpeas, used in South Asian cuisine.

IMMUNE SYSTEM
The organs and processes in the body that help to protect you against infection, such as viruses.

JAIN
Someone who practises Jainism, an ancient faith from India.

LACTOSE
A sugar found in milk and dairy products.

MESOAMERICA
An area around Mexico and Central America in historical times.

NON-ORGANIC
1) Something that isn't alive and never has been.
2) Food that has been grown using chemicals.

OLMEC PEOPLE
The oldest-known civilisation in Mesoamerica, ranging from around 2500 BCE to 400 BCE.

PALM OIL
Edible oil from the fruit of the palm tree. It is a versatile oil but its production can lead to deforestation, where forests are cut down to grow it as a crop.

RHIZOME
A fleshy plant 'stem' that grows underground and sprouts shoots from 'buds'.

SILK ROAD
A network of ancient land routes used by merchants to transport goods between Asian and Middle Eastern countries and Europe. It was used for more than 1,500 years, from around 130 BCE to 1453 CE.

STAPLE FOOD
A type of food that is eaten in such large quantities that it forms a dominant part of a community's diet.

STONE AGE
A prehistoric period when humans used stones to fashion tools. It began roughly 2.6 million years ago and lasted until about 3300 BCE.

TARO
A large-leaved root vegetable grown in tropical regions of the world.

TEOSINTE
A Mexican grass that many people believe to be a parent of modern corn.

TOFU
A soft, soybean curd used in many Asian cuisines including Chinese, Thai, Japanese and Korean cookery.

TUBERS
Fleshy, root-like organs that some plants, such as potatoes and yams, use to store nutrients.

VEGAN
Someone who does not eat or use animal products, in a practice called veganism.

VEGETABLE
The edible parts of a plant that don't contain seeds, such as leaves, roots and stems.

VITAMINS
Organic nutrients that are essential to the human body.

BREAD RECIPE

People have made bread for thousands of years. There are almost as many recipes for it as there are bakers but the basic ingredients and techniques are very similar. This version uses dried yeast which is bought in sachets or small tins.

INGREDIENTS

- 500 g of 'strong' (bread) flour*
- 1 teaspoon of salt
- 300 ml warm (not hot) water
- 1 tablespoon of olive oil
- 1 tablespoon honey
- 1 ½ teaspoons or one sachet of dried yeast

* Contains gluten, but you can swap for gluten-free flour.

Always make sure an adult is with you when cooking.

WHAT TO DO

1. Wash your hands well. If you have one, put on an apron to cover your clothes.

2. Put all the 'dry' ingredients – flour, salt and yeast – into a bowl and briefly stir to mix them up.

3. Add the oil and honey to the warm water and stir them.

4. Pour the liquid into the bowl with the dry ingredients and mix everything together with your hand. It will gradually form a sticky lump (dough). Keep mixing until the lump has included all the bits. The bowl should be almost clean.

5. Sprinkle some flour onto a work surface and knead the dough – stretch it out, fold it back on itself and push it down with your palm. Keep going until it is soft, stretchy and smooth. You may have to add a little more flour.

6. Put the dough back into the bowl and cover with a damp tea towel. Leave it somewhere warm (not the oven!) for about an hour. The dough should nearly double in size.

7. Heat the oven to 400° Fahrenheit, 200° Celsius (180° Celsius fan oven) or Gas mark 6.

8. Form the dough into a simple round or oblong shape and cut a couple of slits in the top. Put it on a lightly oiled baking tray and bake for about 30 to 35 minutes until the loaf is golden.